COUNCIL *on*
FOREIGN
RELATIONS

Discussion Paper
May 2019

Women and Terrorism
Hidden Threats, Forgotten Partners

Jamille Bigio and Rachel Vogelstein

The Council on Foreign Relations (CFR) is an independent, nonpartisan membership organization, think tank, and publisher dedicated to being a resource for its members, government officials, business executives, journalists, educators and students, civic and religious leaders, and other interested citizens in order to help them better understand the world and the foreign policy choices facing the United States and other countries. Founded in 1921, CFR carries out its mission by maintaining a diverse membership, including special programs to promote interest and develop expertise in the next generation of foreign policy leaders; convening meetings at its headquarters in New York and in Washington, DC, and other cities where senior government officials, members of Congress, global leaders, and prominent thinkers come together with CFR members to discuss and debate major international issues; supporting a Studies Program that fosters independent research, enabling CFR scholars to produce articles, reports, and books and hold roundtables that analyze foreign policy issues and make concrete policy recommendations; publishing *Foreign Affairs*, the preeminent journal of international affairs and U.S. foreign policy; sponsoring Independent Task Forces that produce reports with both findings and policy prescriptions on the most important foreign policy topics; and providing up-to-date information and analysis about world events and American foreign policy on its website, CFR.org.

The Council on Foreign Relations takes no institutional positions on policy issues and has no affiliation with the U.S. government. All views expressed in its publications and on its website are the sole responsibility of the author or authors.

For further information about CFR or this paper, please write to the Council on Foreign Relations, 58 East 68th Street, New York, NY 10065, or call Communications at 212.434.9888. Visit CFR's website, CFR.org.

CONTENTS

INTRODUCTION

Extremist groups rely upon women to gain strategic advantage, recruiting them as facilitators and martyrs while also benefiting from their subjugation. Yet U.S. policymakers overlook the roles that women play in violent extremism—including as perpetrators, mitigators, and victims—and rarely enlist their participation in efforts to combat radicalization. This omission puts the United States at a disadvantage in its efforts to prevent terrorism globally and within its borders.

The number of women implicated in terrorism-related crimes is growing. In 2017, the Global Extremism Monitor registered 100 distinct suicide attacks conducted by 181 female militants, 11 percent of all incidents that year. In 2016, women constituted 26 percent of those arrested on terrorism charges in Europe, up from 18 percent the year before. While counterterrorism efforts have reduced the physical stronghold previously held by the Islamic State group, women fuel extremists' continued influence by advancing their ideology online and by indoctrinating their families. New technology allows for more sophisticated outreach, directly targeting messages to radicalize and recruit women. It also provides a platform on which female extremists thrive by expanding their recruitment reach and taking on greater operational roles in the virtual sphere. The failure of counterterrorist efforts to understand the ways in which women radicalize, support, and perpetrate violence cedes the benefit of their involvement to extremist groups.

Omitting women from terrorism prevention efforts also forfeits their potential contributions as mitigators of extremism. Women are well positioned to detect early signs of radicalization, because fundamentalists often target women's rights first. As security officials, women provide insights and information that can be mission critical in keeping the peace. And because of their distinctive access and influence, women are crucial antiterrorism messengers in schools, religious institutions, social environments, and local government. Overlooking the contributions women can make to prevent extremism renders the United States less secure.

Many extremist groups promote an ideology that classifies women as second-class citizens and offers strategic and financial benefits through women's subjugation. Boko Haram, the Islamic State, al-Qaeda, al-Shabab, and other groups use sexual violence to terrorize populations into compliance, displace civilians from strategic areas, enforce unit cohesion among fighters, and even generate revenue through trafficking. Suppressing women's rights also allows extremists to control reproduction and harness female labor.

U.S. government policy and programs continue to underestimate the important roles women can play as perpetrators, mitigators, or targets of violent extremism. Although successive Republican and Democratic administrations have taken modest steps to address women's roles in terrorism, more action is needed. To help prevent and reduce terrorism, the Donald J. Trump administration should produce a National Intelligence Estimate to analyze the ways in which women provide material support to extremist groups; increase resources to facilitate women's involvement in terrorism prevention efforts; and improve the recruitment, retention, and advancement of women across the security sector to bolster the capacity of forces to mitigate potential terrorist threats. These steps will help the United States and its allies respond effectively to the security threat posed by violent extremism and advance U.S. peace and stability.

UNDERSTANDING WOMEN'S ROLES IN TERRORISM

Understanding and addressing women's paths to radicalization and the roles they play in violent extremism is crucial to disrupting terrorists' abilities to recruit, deploy, and abuse them. To reduce the evolving terrorist threat at home and abroad, U.S. counterterrorism strategy should recognize and address the roles of women as perpetrators, mitigators, and targets of violent extremism.

PERPETRATORS

Throughout history, women have joined and supported violent extremist groups, serving as combatants, recruiters, and fundraisers and in numerous other roles critical to operational success. Although women are often ignored in conventional depictions of violent political actors, they have been active participants in 60 percent of armed rebel groups over the past several decades.[1] In Algeria, for instance, female National Liberation Front fighters evaded checkpoints in the 1950s to deploy bombs at strategic urban targets. In Sri Lanka in the 1990s, all-female battalions earned a reputation for their fierce discipline and ruthless combat. Women represented nearly 40 percent of the Revolutionary Armed Forces of Columbia (FARC), serving in all operational roles, including as combat unit leaders, allowing the group to vastly expand its military capacity.[2]

Women have also helped found militant groups, from Germany's Baader-Meinhof gang to the Japanese Red Army. Even in cases where women's leadership was invisible, they frequently provided operationally critical support, ranging from weapons transport to combatant recruitment. Women have also contributed to the normalization of violence: between 1921 and 1931, for example, the women's wing of the Ku

Klux Klan attracted a membership of more than half a million, and their participation in widespread lynching campaigns made targeted political violence more acceptable and even respectable in some communities.[3]

Violence

Today, women-led attacks are on the rise. Several all-female extremist cells have been disrupted in recent years, from a group of ten women in Morocco found obtaining chemicals used to make explosives, to a woman and her two daughters in London plotting to attack tourists at the British Museum.[4] Female members of Boko Haram have been so effective—killing more than 1,200 people between 2014 and 2018—that women now comprise close to two-thirds of the group's suicide attackers.[5] Attacks by women have been growing not only in number but also in severity. In Nigeria, the most deadly incident in 2018 involved three women bombers who killed twenty people in a crowded marketplace.[6] In Indonesia, the deadliest attacks in decades were carried out by two family units that included both women and children.[7] Female suicide attacks are more lethal on average than those conducted by men: according to one study of five different terrorist groups, attacks carried out by women had an average of 8.4 victims—compared to 5.3 for attacks carried out by men—and were less likely to fail.[8]

While some women are kidnapped and forcibly conscripted into violence, many voluntarily join extremist groups for reasons similar to those of male recruits, including ideological commitment or social ties.[9] Others join in hopes of gaining freedom and access to resources; in Nigeria, for example, some women joined Boko Haram to receive Koranic education in a region where only 4 percent of girls have the opportunity to finish secondary school.[10]

Recruitment and Operational Support

Women also participate in recruitment, fundraising, propaganda dissemination, and other forms of material support for violent extremism. In 2014, a network of fifteen women across the United States was charged for transferring thousands of dollars to al-Shabab militants in Somalia, using small transactions and coded language to avoid detection.[11] Palestinian women have been arrested for running fraudulent charitable organizations that funneled money to the Palestinian Islamic Jihad. In Indonesia, police identified a pattern of women marrying foreign Islamic State fighters and then remaining in the country to fundraise. And in Pakistan, wives of Jemaah Islamiyah leaders served as the group's bookkeepers and managed significant fundraising efforts.[12]

Women also play a wide variety of auxiliary roles that can be integral to the operational success of extremist groups. Armed insurgencies abetted by women control more territory and are more likely to achieve victory over government forces, in part because women's participation signals greater community support, increases perceived legitimacy, and contributes to tactical effectiveness.[13] Radical white nationalist leaders across multiple groups in the United States have commented that women's participation stabilizes membership, and that women are more likely to remain as members than men.[14] For insurgencies or terrorist groups focused on state-building, such as the Islamic State, women carry out essential tasks that bolster capacity, like feeding and clothing combatants, transporting weapons, and educating new recruits. Across ideologies, women play a crucial role in indoctrinating their families, facilitating both radicalization and terrorist recruitment.[15] In Islamic State–held territory, for example, women raised the children they had brought with them and gave birth to over seven hundred more as part of a strategy to grow the caliphate.[16]

Modern extremist groups use social media to actively enlist women into supportive roles, reaching unprecedented numbers through narrowcasting—creating a targeted message for a specific subgroup.[17] For instance, the Islamic State's concerted campaign to recruit Western women emphasized camaraderie, sisterhood, and opportunities to enjoy freedom and adventure as state-builders.[18] Nearly 20 percent of Western recruits to the Islamic State are female, a markedly higher rate than in other Islamist jihadi groups.[19]

Once enlisted, women are also especially effective as recruiters: one study of online pro–Islamic State groups found that female recruiters had higher network connectivity than men, making them more effective at spreading the Islamic State's message than their male counterparts— an important finding given that an increasing number of extremists are radicalized online. Women's participation also improved the survival rate of online pro–Islamic State groups, extending the time before technology companies shut them down.[20]

Accountability and Reintegration

Criminal justice responses often fail to address the diverse roles that female members of extremist groups hold. Many female members of the Islamic State joined voluntarily and played active roles in recruiting tens of thousands of foreign fighters to the cause. However, after women voluntarily join, some are required to remain against their will and coerced into continued service.[21] Local women in Iraq and Syria, for instance, often found themselves coerced into service for the Islamic State in order to survive when their homes were overtaken by militias.

Other women are targeted and trafficked into extremist groups and forced to perpetrate crimes. Boko Haram strategically kidnapped young girls and teenagers and forced many into suicide missions, raising questions about their agency and accountability.[22] Other trafficking victims, however, become sympathetic to the group after exposure to its ideology.[23] Some female members of Boko Haram who had initially been forced into service decided to stay in the group voluntarily after finding they had access to resources and power unavailable to them in their home communities.[24]

Despite the complexities of women's roles in violence, officials in criminal justice systems around the world often assume that women who commit violence are either naive victims of circumstance or dangerous deviants from the natural order. Correspondingly, approaches to women's repatriation and reintegration vary significantly with respect to their criminal and civil accountability.[25]

Criminal justice leaders sometimes view women as casualties of terrorism regardless of their motivation, resulting in fewer arrests for terrorism-related crimes and shorter-than-average sentences.[26] This phenomenon has occurred across the United States and Europe; in the Balkans, governments do not account for noncombatant support provided by female affiliates of the Islamic State, and most female returnees avoid prosecution altogether.[27]

In other cases, officials in criminal justice systems have imposed overly harsh consequences for female returnees as compared to their male counterparts. German courts have charged women returning from Syria with war crimes while indicting men under domestic terrorism legislation.[28] Although the United States and the United Kingdom have permitted many male foreign fighters to return and face trial, both governments refused reentry of female Islamic State affiliates—including Shamima Begum and Hoda Muthana—and revoked their citizenship. In Iraq, female Islamic State affiliates face the harshest possible punishments—death or life in prison—even when the women have not been involved in violent acts and argued they had been coerced into traveling to Islamic State territory.[29]

Once female extremists are identified, prison and rehabilitation programs designed for men fail to address the underlying causes of women's radicalization.[30] Women who joined violent political groups such as the FARC in Colombia and the Sri Lankan Liberation Tigers of Tamil Eelam reported that membership provided greater freedom than could be found in traditional society.[31] When female fighters return to communities where social norms remain unchanged, they sometimes rejoin extremist groups, a trend observed with female members of Boko Haram in Nigeria and FARC women in Colombia (who were less likely to demobilize than male members between 2003 and 2012).[32] Furthermore, programs often fail to provide training in livelihood skills that could help women support themselves and their children, instead offering training in stereotypically feminine, low-wage activities such as hairstyling and sewing.[33] And few programs provide adequate services for women's specific needs, such as appropriate support for victims of trauma or sexual violence.[34]

Children also complicate the reintegration of female returnees. In some cases, communities that are willing to embrace returnees refuse to accept descendants of terrorists.[35] For children born in war zones, issues of citizenship present a serious challenge for social services, and states have not reached consensus about responsibility for and repatriation of this population.[36] And as their parents await judgment, many children languish in dire conditions. Some children, including Shamima Begum's infant son, have died in custody.[37]

As governments determine their approaches toward repatriating and holding accountable Islamic State–affiliated women, thousands wait in Iraqi displacement camps.[38] Without either a comprehensive criminal justice response or sufficient resources for rehabilitation, returning women are likely to fall through the cracks.

MITIGATORS

Women are already on the front lines when it comes to preventing and countering violent extremism in their communities. Yet their voices remain sidelined from mainstream counterterrorism debates. Incorporating women's distinctive perspectives can lead to better intelligence gathering and more targeted responses to potential security threats. Women-led civil society groups are particularly critical partners in mitigating violence, though counterterrorism efforts too often fail to enlist them.

Predictors

Women are well positioned to recognize early signs of radicalization because attacks on their rights and physical autonomy are often the first indication of a rise in fundamentalism. Women are substantially more likely than men to be early victims of extremism, through harassment in public spaces, forced segregation, dress requirements, attacks on girls' schooling, and other violations.[39]

Women's central roles in many families and communities also afford them a unique vantage point from which to recognize unusual patterns of behavior and forecast impending conflict. In Afghanistan, women observed that young men were being recruited at weddings; after their concerns went unheeded, these recruits killed thirty-two civilians on a bus.[40] In Libya, local women warned of rising radicalism after observing an increased flow of Western female recruits, signaling a growing market for wives as the Islamic State expanded its stronghold. They also reported rising attacks on their own rights, including harassment for driving without a male guardian.[41] As in Afghanistan, these warnings were disregarded, providing the Islamic State leaders additional time to establish a headquarters before counterterrorism efforts ramped up.

Security Actors

Female security officials provide distinct insights and information that can be mission critical. Women serving as security leaders are able to conduct searches of female fighters in ways that men often cannot; strategically deploying women can thereby prevent extremists from evading screening. Female security officials also have access to populations and sites that men do not, allowing them to gather critical intelligence about potential security threats.[42] Furthermore, women's participation in the military and police has been shown to improve how a local community perceives law enforcement, which, in turn, improves their ability to provide security.[43]

The underrepresentation of women in security roles, however, creates a vulnerability that terrorist groups exploit to their advantage. Women comprise just 15 percent of police forces globally; in South Asia, women make up less than 2 percent of the force in Pakistan, less than 7 percent in Bangladesh, and less than 8 percent in India.[44] Female combatants can hide suicide devices under their clothing knowing that they are unlikely to encounter a female security official and therefore will not be searched. Without efforts to improve gender gaps in national security roles, female extremists will retain an advantage in eluding suspicion and arrest.

Preventers

Traditional efforts by governments and nongovernmental organizations to combat radicalization typically focus on outreach to predominantly male political and religious leaders. However, the prominent role that many women play in their families and communities renders them especially effective in diminishing the ability of extremist groups to recruit and mobilize.[45] Women are well positioned to challenge extremist narratives in homes, schools, and social environments. Women have particular influence among youth populations, a frequent target of extremists. In more conservative societies—where communicating with women is limited to other women or their male relatives—women have unique access to intervene with women and girls at risk of radicalization.[46]

Small-scale efforts to involve women show promise. A program in Morocco deploys women religious scholars around the country to counter radical interpretations of Islam—they were better able to reach community members than their male counterparts because of their social ties and ability to build trust.[47] In Nigeria, an interfaith group of Muslim and Christian women came together in the wake of an extremist attack and successfully supported community policing efforts in regions with high levels of intercommunity violence.[48] An Indonesian program provided wives of incarcerated jihadis with psychological and economic support, which helped them rehabilitate and reintegrate formerly violent combatants into their community, breaking the cycle of extremism.[49]

Despite the important role women can play as preventers of terrorism, women's groups are rarely considered relevant partners in counterterrorism efforts, and their work remains chronically underfunded. Furthermore, when counterterrorism officials develop policy without input from local women, they risk entrenching harmful social norms about women's place in society that undermine women's rights.[50] In addition, regulations intended to cut down on terrorist financing are making it harder for women's groups—including those that work against radicalization—to function.[51] Women's civil society organizations are typically smaller and less financially resilient, making it difficult for many of them to meet the compliance requirements associated with counterterrorist financing regimes. In some instances, governments from Egypt to Russia have criminalized feminist activity in the name of counterterrorism, targeting women's civil society organizations that challenge the status quo in their countries.[52] Ensuring that women's groups can receive funding without falling afoul of antiterrorism laws would increase their contributions to counterterrorism efforts, while also fulfilling the state's obligations under international law to ensure nondiscrimination and equality.

TARGETS

Many extremist groups benefit both strategically and financially from the subjugation of women. A number of terrorist groups use human trafficking as a means to recruit new members and finance their operations.[53] The Islamic State systematically bought and sold women and girls through sales contracts notarized by Islamic State–run courts.[54] The group attracted thousands of male recruits by offering kidnapped women and girls as "wives," and generated significant revenue through sex trafficking, sexual slavery, and extortion through ransom.[55] The United Nations estimated that ransom payments extracted by the Islamic State amounted to between $35 million and $45 million in 2013 alone.[56] This practice is deployed by other terrorist groups as well: in northern Nigeria and the Lake Chad region, Boko Haram abducts women and girls as a deliberate tactic to generate payments through ransom, exchange prisoners, or lure security forces to an ambush.[57] Some of these kidnapped girls are then coerced into suicide attacks; in fact, one in three of Boko Haram's female suicide bombers is a minor.[58] Sexual violence is also a tactical tool to enforce population compliance, socialize combatants and encourage unit cohesion, displace civilians from strategic areas, and drive instability.[59]

Not only is violence against women and girls a tactic of violent extremists, but it is also a potential warning sign for mass killings. A third of individuals associated with jihadi-inspired attacks inside the United States had a record of domestic abuse or other sexual violence.[60] In the United States, a study of FBI data on mass shootings between 2009 and 2015 found that 57 percent of victims included a spouse, former spouse, or family member, and that in 16 percent of cases, the attackers had a history of perpetrating domestic violence.[61]

The stigma associated with sexual violence waged by extremists remains a potent force that marginalizes women in the economic sphere and can result in isolation and a loss of marriage prospects, leading to a lifetime of poverty.[62] Children born of rape frequently experience discrimination and exclusion from services: offspring of girls captured by Boko Haram are stigmatized as having "bad blood" and are significantly more likely to be abused and uneducated.[63] Survivors of physical and psychological trauma often struggle to recover, and the ramifications compound across generations.[64]

The use of sexual violence and subjugation of women serves an additional tactical purpose of manipulating perceptions of masculinity to recruit men. Extremist groups whose ideologies subjugate women reinforce oppressive gender roles and promise men supremacy, respect, and sexual partners.[65] Such groups promise an alternative path to manhood when social or economic markers of masculinity are not available.[66] For example, these groups can provide wives for men in societies where economic barriers, including high bride price, put marriage out of reach, a phenomenon that is linked to broader social instability and susceptibility to radicalization.[67]

COUNTRY PROFILES

Evaluating how women perpetrate and prevent terrorism in different countries demonstrates their centrality to counterterrorism programs and policy. Efforts to increase women's participation in police forces in Afghanistan illustrate how they improve operational effectiveness, as well as the social and cultural barriers they face. Terrorist activity in Nigeria demonstrates the varied roles women play—including as perpetrators, mitigators, and targets—and how ignoring their contributions undermines security efforts. Women's experiences in Northern Ireland exemplify the long history of women's involvement in perpetrating political violence and countering extremism. And in the United States, women's radicalization and participation in violent extremism at home and abroad is on the rise, paralleled by women's leadership in the intelligence community and security sectors.

Afghanistan

In Afghanistan, efforts to recruit and train more female police officers have highlighted the ways in which women can strengthen counterterrorism efforts—as well as the challenges they face. Female officers are tasked with searching women and children during raids and at checkpoints, filling a critical security gap.[68] In neighboring Pakistan, policewomen are often seconded to the army to help with counterinsurgency operations, because security forces' entering private homes without a female officer would alienate the local community and undermine their capacity to understand and anticipate extremist threats.[69]

Recognizing this, in 2013, the U.S. Congress designated a minimum of $25 million in the National Defense Authorization Act to support women in the Afghan security forces.[70] At the time, women comprised only 1 percent of the Afghan National Police. Today, the North Atlantic Treaty Organization (NATO)–led mission to train and assist Afghan security forces aims to increase women's representation to 10 percent by 2021.[71] However, increasing the proportion of women demands more than recruitment, as women who join the police force face serious challenges, including social stigma from their communities, sexual harassment from colleagues, and targeted violence because of their easily recognized uniforms.[72] There are also few opportunities for women's advancement in the police force, which the Afghan government is addressing through creating women-only positions and eliminating limitations on the types of jobs women can hold.[73] Recruiting and retaining female security officers will require significant efforts to improve educational and training opportunities, address internal harassment and discrimination, and shift social and cultural norms.

Nigeria

In 2014, Boko Haram, a jihadi group allied with the Islamic State, made global headlines after kidnapping 276 Chibok schoolgirls, resulting in an international effort to attain their release. Following the abduction, Boko Haram began a widespread campaign using female suicide bombers, including several girls they had forcibly recruited. Between 2014 and 2018, more than 450 women and girls were deployed in suicide attacks; at least a third of them were teenagers or young children.[74] These female suicide bombers have been so effective—killing more than 1,200 people over just four years—that today women comprise close to two-thirds of the group's suicide attackers.[75] Their success is due in part to their exploiting the gender gap in the Nigerian security forces, which lack female security officials to search women.

Efforts to deradicalize and rehabilitate female Boko Haram combatants reveal the complexity of women's roles in terrorist groups. Women who were initially abducted sometimes shift their roles to better their situation, because of personal relationships, or because of indoctrination of radical ideas. Other women report voluntarily joining the terrorist group because of social or political pressures, or for economic opportunities offered by Boko Haram that were not available in their conservative communities.[76] In parts of Nigeria that have been devastated by government and militia violence, women who return from Boko Haram receive little socioeconomic support and often face stigma, sexual violence, and poverty.[77] Their families and communities sometimes view them with suspicion, and their children born of militants are more likely to be abused or remain uneducated.[78] These factors fuel an intergenerational cycle of extremism, leading some women to rejoin Boko Haram and leaving their children vulnerable to radicalization.

To address this complexity, female civil society leaders have launched grassroots initiatives, partnering with local leaders, governments, and security officials to combat radicalization and build community resilience. The Allamin Foundation for Peace and Development provides comprehensive support to former wives, abductees, and combatants affiliated with Boko Haram. In concert with Islamic scholars, the foundation developed counter-narratives that have been deployed through radio programs and resulted in a 40 percent increase in children's enrollment in public schools.[79] Psychologist Fatima Akilu's Neem Foundation builds community management teams comprising security officials, faith leaders, and women's organizations, offering tools and networks to help identify and deter radicalization. Mobile counseling units provide psychological services for displaced communities, addressing the isolation on which recruiters prey.[80]

Northern Ireland

From the 1960s to the 1990s, Northern Ireland was immersed in a political conflict known as the Troubles, which resulted in more than 1,800 civilian deaths from cross fire between British security forces and paramilitary groups.[81] Women were active participants in supporting and sustaining terrorist violence on both the nationalist and unionist sides. The Irish Republican Army (IRA) celebrated women's participation by featuring prominent martyrs such as Maire Drumm and Mairead Farrell in group propaganda.[82] Some of these women deployed gender-specific tactics: in 1990, a young IRA militant concealed explosives under the guise of a late-term pregnancy. Although she was caught on her way to place the bomb at the Belfast airport, the tactic was copied by others in Northern Ireland and around the world.[83] Women also actively disrupted counterinsurgency efforts: in response to arbitrary raids and arrests, women in Catholic neighborhoods established regular patrols and banged pots and pans to warn nationalist militants of approaching security forces.[84] Though women were less visible in unionist paramilitaries, the Ulster Defence Association included up to two dozen women's units.[85]

Northern Irish women also laid cross-community foundations for a successful peace agreement in 1998. Notable women-led groups, including Derry Peace Women, Peace People, and Women Together, mobilized thousands of men and women in public protest demanding an end to paramilitary violence.[86] Their pressure was a critical factor in bringing parties to the table for serious negotiations. The Northern Ireland Women's Coalition played an important role in the successful Good Friday process, ensuring that potential deal breakers were incorporated into the talks and advocating for human rights provisions to prevent future extremist violence.[87]

United States

Domestically, violent political organizations across the ideological spectrum rely on female recruitment.[88] Women extremists have perpetrated deadly attacks in the homeland, notably Islamist Tashfeen Malik, the attacker in the 2015 San Bernardino, California, attack.[89] Over the last twenty years, the number of female supporters of far-right groups has grown drastically; women have played a particularly important role in spreading extremist ideas online.[90] Women also have a critical presence among American jihadis, especially in developing recruitment networks.[91] One of the first American jihadi travelers—and the first known American to have been killed in Syria—was Nicole Lynn Mansfield, a woman from Flint, Michigan.[92]

Radicalized American women tend to commit the same types of crimes and have about the same success rate as radicalized men.[93] Yet they are less likely to be arrested and convicted, and they ultimately serve shorter-than-average sentences for terrorism-related crimes, highlighting a discrepancy in treatment and leaving a security threat unaddressed.[94] The phenomenon of American women who have become Islamic State affiliates now hoping to return to the United States raises significant questions about accountability and reintegration into American society.

U.S. women have also ascended to leadership roles in the counterterrorism field across administrations, including service as secretaries of homeland security, White House homeland security advisors, CIA directors, and senior intelligence officials. Women currently hold many top CIA positions and comprise about a third of the Senior Intelligence Service.[95] Some of the intelligence community's most critical missions have been led by women; more than half the analysts in Alec Station, the team charged with finding Osama bin Laden, were women.[96] And many have lost their lives on the job, such as Jennifer Matthews, one of the CIA's top al-Qaeda experts, who was killed in a bombing in Afghanistan, and Shannon Kent, who served alongside special operations forces to target Islamic State leaders until her death in Syria in 2019.[97]

At the community level, American women are leading prevention and intervention programs, bringing a gender lens to domestic reintegration work. Angela King, cofounder of Life After Hate, is a former far-right extremist leader who created woman-centric propaganda before her arrest in 1998. Since her release from prison, she has worked to counter extremism through public awareness campaigns and individual support for those exiting white nationalist movements.[98]

POLICY CONSIDERATIONS FOR THE UNITED STATES

In recent years, as evidence of women's contributions to perpetrating and preventing violent extremist activity has grown, the United States has begun to pay closer attention to the role of women in preventing terrorism. Yet more can and should be done to incorporate women into U.S. strategies to combat the threat of terrorism at home and abroad. To safeguard U.S. security interests, the country's counterterrorism policy should mitigate the danger posed by female extremists while involving women from the outset as partners in the fight against terrorism.

CURRENT U.S. AND GLOBAL POLICY

Over the past three consecutive presidential administrations, the U.S. government has taken steps to grow women's participation in counterterrorism efforts, yet most advances on this issue have remained detached from broader counterterrorism policy and initiatives, leading to insufficient resourcing. Drawing on lessons from the George W. Bush administration's programs that invested in women leaders as counterterrorism partners, the Barack Obama administration issued a series of policies—including the 2011 U.S. National Action Plan on Women, Peace, and Security and its 2016 revision, and the 2016 joint U.S. State Department–U.S. Agency for International Development (USAID) strategy to counter violent extremism—that referenced women's contributions as critical to combating violent extremism.[99] The bipartisan Women, Peace, and Security Act of 2017—signed into law by President Trump—echoes this commitment, although it remains to be seen how the Trump administration's forthcoming Women, Peace, and Security strategy to implement the act will address this issue.

The most substantive policy to date was developed in 2019 by the State Department and USAID per congressional request, and outlined commitments to support women and girls at risk from extremism and conflict. However, these commitments have been generally absent from broader U.S. counterterrorism policy, including the 2011 and 2018 U.S. National Strategies for Counterterrorism, which largely ignore women. And while earmarked funding has supported women and girls at risk from extremism, it represents only a negligible fraction of the broader budget for counterterrorism, resulting in many missed opportunities where women's contributions could have improved the effectiveness of U.S. operations. To address this gap, a bipartisan group in the U.S. House of Representatives introduced legislation in 2019 to require U.S. counterterrorism policy to address the roles that women play as perpetrators, mitigators, and victims of terrorism.

Although the United States has taken steps in recent years to grow the number of women in national security positions, their representation remains uneven across departments and agencies. A lack of diversity in the U.S. national security apparatus handicaps its ability to effectively detect and deter female combatants. Women hold about a third of the senior roles at the State Department and CIA, but at the Defense Department they comprise only 16 percent of active duty forces and hold fewer than 10 percent of leadership positions.[100] In Congress, only one member of the Senate Foreign Relations Committee is a woman (5 percent), and women comprise just 15 percent of the House Foreign Affairs Committee. Women represent approximately 20 percent of both the House and Senate Intelligence Committees, and almost a third of the Senate Armed Services and Homeland Security and Governmental Affairs Committees.

In parallel to progress in U.S. policy, other governments and multilateral organizations around the world have begun to appreciate the critical importance of women's participation in counterterrorism efforts. In 2015, the United Nations adopted Security Council Resolution 2242, the first to focus on the implications of women's roles in both perpetrating and countering terrorism. Since then, gender considerations have been mainstreamed throughout UN counterterrorism bodies and policies, including the secretary-general's Plan of Action to Prevent Violent Extremism and the 2018 Global Counterterrorism Strategy, both of which urge member states to prioritize women's radicalization. The Global Counterterrorism Forum—a multilateral body comprising twenty-nine countries and the European Union, aimed at preventing, combating, and prosecuting terrorism—now hosts a working group on countering violent extremism focused on women's roles and the influence of gender.[101] And the Organization for Security and Cooperation in Europe has provided comprehensive guidelines on how its nearly sixty participating states from across Central Asia, Europe, and North America can integrate gender considerations in national responses to violent extremism.

Some nations have adopted explicit policies to recognize women's roles in counterterrorism, but as with the U.S. government's approach, these policies are usually disjointed from broader security initiatives and lack resources for implementation. The United Kingdom committed to deploy women to amplify prevention measures at the community level in its 2011 national counterterrorism policy. In 2015, the League of Arab States agreed to a regional plan on women's involvement in peace and security efforts that includes a focus on terrorism response, an approach that has been reflected in national plans across the region. Jordan's plan, for instance, seeks to combat radicalization through the meaningful participation of women in counterterrorism efforts.[102] In Africa, both Kenya and Somalia issued counterterrorism strategies that recognize gender as a factor in violent extremism and promote gender equality to increase resiliency against terror.[103] Yet several national action plans on preventing violent extremism, including those from Finland and Norway, do not even mention women.[104] These policy gaps are accompanied by resource gaps that, like in the United States, leave counterterrorism forces at a disadvantage.

Counterterrorism policies that underestimate or ignore the role women play as perpetrators, mitigators, and victims of terrorism jeopardize U.S. security interests and cede a strategic advantage to terrorist organizations. As part of the Trump administration's commitment to advancing U.S. security interests, the U.S. government should increase its support for women's contributions to combating extremism.

Critics could allege that gender-neutral counterterrorism efforts are effective, targeting the most dangerous extremists—men or women— and that a specific focus on women will distract from this goal. However, evidence suggests that gender-blind approaches risk susceptibility to stereotypes that allow female fighters to evade counterterrorism efforts, and fail to recognize the noncombatant support roles often held by women. Gender-neutral approaches can hamper prevention efforts through overreliance on community leaders who are predominantly male, thereby overlooking the capacity of women who wield considerable influence in their homes and communities. Furthermore, this argument obscures the fact that gender already influences U.S. risk assessments that focus on military-age males.

Others will question the diversion of resources to focus on women and gender at a time of significant security challenges at home and abroad and restricted budgets, especially given that men remain more likely than women to hold combatant roles. However, assumptions and long-standing stereotypes obscure both the rising number of women who serve as perpetrators and the critical role women play in support capacities or as victims of violence that aids and abets the success of terrorist groups. To improve program effectiveness and reduce extremism, a greater commitment of resources is needed to understand the complex ways in which gender affects recruitment, radicalization, and reintegration—for both men and women—as well as greater attention to women's roles in terrorism.

To strengthen U.S. efforts to prevent terrorism and promote stability, the White House—together with the intelligence community, the Departments of Defense, Justice, State, and Treasury, and USAID— should both address the security risk posed by female extremists and increase the role of women in its counterterrorism efforts. The United States also should lead by example by taking meaningful steps to include women in domestic efforts to protect the homeland.

Congress should encourage these steps and provide oversight by passing legislation. For example, House bill 1653 on women and countering violent extremism would ensure that U.S. policy and programs address the roles women play as perpetrators, preventers, and victims of terrorism.

Combat the Sources of Terrorist Support

The director of national intelligence should produce a National Intelligence Estimate. Diminishing the capacity of terrorists to conduct attacks requires addressing the many and varied forms of support women provide to extremist groups. To better understand the ways in which women facilitate and support extremist groups, the director of national intelligence should produce a National Intelligence Estimate and form an operational task force on the relationship between women, violent extremism, and terrorism, including an analysis of women's roles as recruiters, sympathizers, perpetrators, and combatants.

The Departments of State and Treasury should block extremist groups' access to assets raised through abduction for trafficking, trading, and sexual exploitation. Regarding continued material support for the Islamic State, the State and Treasury Departments should work with partners in the Global Coalition to Defeat ISIS to provide technical assistance to the Iraqi government to locate the estimated three thousand Yazidi women and girls—members of a religious minority targeted and kidnapped by the Islamic State—still enslaved and used to profit the group.[105]

Address Radicalization and Recruitment

The United States should establish an advisory council on preventing terrorism that includes a focus on women's roles in perpetrating and preventing terrorism. The U.S. government's implementation of its national counterterrorism strategy should capitalize on women's full participation in preventing and countering violent extremism, including by addressing gender-specific drivers of radicalization and terrorist recruitment strategies. To assist this effort, the U.S. secretary of state, in consultation with the secretary of defense, the CIA director, and the USAID administrator, should create an advisory council on terrorism that recognizes women's roles. In addition, to increase program effectiveness, U.S.-funded counterterrorism organizations should regularly consult women leaders to shape prevention, deradicalization, and rehabilitation programs, recognizing that terrorist efforts to radicalize, recruit, and mobilize new members often rely on gendered narratives and stereotypes.

The United States should target messages to women at risk of radicalization. Such messages have been effective, such as in South and Southeast Asia, where Mythos Labs developed short YouTube videos with local social influencers and comedians that used humor to parody patriarchal messages in India and poke fun at extremist recruiting practices in Indonesia. The videos were well received and corresponded with a 10 percent reduction in pro–Islamic State tweets from the region over the three weeks after the videos were posted.[106] In Germany, the Lola for Democracy program counters the influence of right-wing extremism and the growing role of female extremists in the movement by advising schools on how to promote counter-messages emphasizing diversity and equality, in addition to training police officers, teachers, and journalists on gender in right-wing extremism.[107]

The U.S. government should build on the 2018 Group of Seven security ministers' commitments on gender and counterterrorism by enlisting the Group of Twenty nations to adopt similar commitments. It also should encourage governments to classify survivors of sexual violence by terrorist or extremist groups as victims of terrorism and thus undermine efforts to isolate victims and weaken communities.

The U.S. intelligence community should overhaul its assessments to include women's rights. Globally, women's rights and physical integrity are often the first targets of fundamentalists. The intelligence community should require data collection of indicators related to women's equality and autonomy as potential early warning signs of growing fundamentalist influence, and should encourage its allies to follow suit.

The State Department's annual country reports on terrorism should include a gender analysis of the factors relevant to violent extremism. The Departments of Defense and State and USAID should conduct or commission at least one research product per fiscal year on gender and preventing terrorism, and ensure that policies and programs are informed by its results.

Increase Partnerships

The U.S. government should invest at least $250 million annually to facilitate women's involvement in terrorism prevention efforts. The United States should direct resources through the Global Community

Engagement and Resilience Fund to support women's efforts to reduce marginalization, counter propaganda, and reintegrate returned foreign terrorist fighters. The United States has provided support for numerous research and program initiatives aimed at partnering with women to counter violent extremism. Now is the time to scale successful initiatives and incorporate them into core counterterrorism programs and budgets.

U.S. security cooperation efforts should provide technical assistance to increase the recruitment, retention, and advancement of women in security sectors. Terrorist and violent extremist groups exploit the absence of women in the security sector. The secretary of state should increase the participation of women in the Department of State's Antiterrorism Assistance program, with the goal of doubling within three years the total number of women receiving training. Furthermore, the U.S. government should require all countries participating in its security and justice programs to send delegations that are at least 30 percent female, a threshold supported by research on representation to facilitate women's inclusion.[108] This target would not only enable additional training opportunities for women who could otherwise be overlooked in the participant selection process, but would also set a norm of male and female national security officials working together. Furthermore, U.S. training and support for police forces should encourage the participation of women in community-police dialogues on counterterrorism.

The U.S. government should help fund a new position proposed by the UN Office of Counterterrorism to expand their outreach to civil society, including women-led organizations. Likewise, Washington should encourage similar outreach by national governments and by the UN Counterterrorism Executive Directorate to capitalize on the information and capacity women offer in preventing extremism.

The U.S. government should encourage the private sector to foster partnerships with women to combat radicalization. For example, when companies provide youth populations at risk of radicalization with vocational training, mentoring, or job opportunities, they should also include targeted support for female youth.[109] In addition, Washington should encourage the technology industry—which has a critical role in countering extremist narratives and messages online—to include more content tailored for women. Google's Redirect Method uses targeted advertising and preexisting YouTube content to divert people looking for extremist content; these efforts would be made stronger by targeting women as well as men.

Women are present in nearly half of all violent political organizations in the United States, ranging from white nationalist militias to environmental extremist groups.[110] Yet law enforcement and the criminal justice system often replicate the same blind spots when working to combat radicalization in the United States.

The Department of Homeland Security should invest $50 million at the state and local government level to prevent women's radicalization. Domestic communication efforts should target messages to reach women, both those at risk of radicalization and those poised to mitigate it. Messages should offer a broad range of interpretations of Islam and draw more broadly on available lessons from the State Department's Global Engagement Center.

The U.S. government should allow all female Islamic State affiliates to return to face trial in U.S. courts. It should simultaneously ensure that the criminal justice system requires accountability for women on an equal basis to men. Federal and state judicial and law enforcement officials involved in terrorism cases should receive training to promote a more nuanced approach to dealing with female extremists that takes into account their agency as well as potential coercion and trauma. U.S. courts should also incorporate lessons from sexual assault prosecution to avoid re-traumatizing victims, witnesses, and other survivors participating in the justice process.

The U.S. government should expand the representation of women across the national security apparatus. Just as female security officials and civil society leaders bring unique advantages to counterterrorism operations across the globe, their perspectives are needed to bring innovative thinking to countering domestic extremism. It should take steps to increase the proportion of women in the U.S. national security sector, from the military and intelligence apparatus to law enforcement, by doubling recruitment, promotion, and retention efforts and maintaining rigorous implementation of antidiscrimination laws. To improve U.S. preparedness and lead by example, the Women, Peace, and Security Act of 2017 should be amended to include prevention of violent extremism and terrorism in required training for U.S. government officials.

The U.S. government should invest in research on women to better understand women's participation in domestic extremist movements. Efforts should include sex-disaggregating the FBI's reported data on perpetrators and supporting academic efforts to collect information on extremists.

CONCLUSION

Given the rise in women's participation in extremist groups, the United States can no longer afford to ignore the ways in which women can strengthen counterterrorism efforts. To improve U.S. counterterrorism strategy, the Trump administration should counter the exploitation of women by extremist groups by involving more women in antiradicalization and recruitment efforts and increasing women's participation in the security sector at home and abroad.

ENDNOTES

1. Alexis Leanna Henshaw, "Where Women Rebel: Patterns of Women's Participation in Armed Rebel Groups 1990–2008," *International Feminist Journal of Politics* 18, no. 1 (2016): 39–60, http://doi.org/10.1080/14616742.2015.1007729; Karla J. Cunningham, "Cross-Regional Trends in Female Terrorism," *Studies in Conflict and Terrorism* 26, no. 3 (2013): 171–195, http://doi.org/10.1080/10576100390211419.

2. Zohra Drif, *Inside the Battle of Algiers*, trans. Andrew Farrand (Charlottesville, VA: Just World Books, 2017); Miranda Alison, "Cogs in the Wheel? Women in the Liberation Tigers of Tamil Eelam," *Civil Wars* 6, no. 4 (Winter 2003): 37–54, http://doi.org/10.1080/13698240308402554; Francisco Gutierez Sanin and Francy Carranza Franco, "Organizing Women for Combat: The Experience of the FARC in the Colombian War," *Journal of Agrarian Change* 17, no. 4 (October 2017), http://doi.org/10.1111/joac.12238.

3. Kathleen M. Blee, "Women and Organized Racial Terrorism in the United States," *Studies in Conflict and Terrorism* 28, no. 5 (2005): 426, http://doi.org/10.1080/10576100500180303.

4. "All-Female 'Islamic State' Cell Arrested in Morocco," Deutsche Welle, March 10, 2016, http://dw.com/en/all-female-islamic-state-cell-arrested-in-morocco/a-35948566; Hayley Dixon, "Teenager in All Female Isil Terror Plot Planned to Attack British Museum," *Telegraph*, May 10, 2018, http://telegraph.co.uk/news/2018/05/10/teenager-female-isil-terror-plot-planned-attack-british-museum.

5. Conor Gaffey, "ISIS Just Started Using Female Suicide Bombers, but Boko Haram Has Been Doing It for Years—and Shows No Sign of Stopping," *Newsweek*, August 12, 2017, http://newsweek.com/isis-boko-haram-nigeria-suicide-bomber-649790; Vladimir Hernandez and Stephanie Hegarty, "Made-Up to Look Beautiful. Sent Out to Die: The Young Women Sent Into Crowds to Blow Themselves Up," BBC News, 2018, http://bbc.co.uk/news/resources/idt-sh/made_up_to_look_beautiful_sent_out_to_die; Jason Warner and Hilary Matfess, "Exploding Stereotypes: The Unexpected Operational and Demographic Characteristics of Boko Haram's Suicide Bombers," Combating Terrorism Center at West Point, August 2017, https://ctc.usma.edu/app/uploads/2017/08/Exploding-Stereotypes-1.pdf.

6. Dionne Searcey, "Three Suicide Bombers Kill at Least 20 in Nigeria," *New York Times*, February 17, 2018, http://nytimes.com/2018/02/17/world/africa/nigeria-suicide -bombing.html.

7. Joseph Hincks, "Indonesia Suffers Its Worst Terrorist Attack in a Decade. Here's What to Know About the Latest Wave of Violence," *Time*, May 14, 2018, http://time.com /5275738/indonesia-suicide-bombings-isis-surabaya.

8. Lindsey O'Rourke, "What's Special About Female Suicide Terrorism?," *Security Studies* 18, no. 4 (2009): 687, http://doi.org/10.1080/09636410903369084.

9. Beverley Milton-Edwards and Sumaya Attia, "Female Terrorists and Their Role in Jihadi Groups," Brookings Institution, May 9, 2017, http://brookings.edu/opinions /female-terrorists-and-their-role-in-jihadi-groups; "Journey to Extremism in Africa: Drivers, Incentives and the Tipping Point for Recruitment," UN Development Program (2017), http://journey-to-extremism.undp.org/content/downloads/UNDP -JourneyToExtremism-report-2017-english.pdf.

10. Hilary Matfess, *Women and the War on Boko Haram: Wives, Weapons, Witnesses* (London: Zed Books, 2017).

11. Audrey Alexander, "Cruel Intentions: Female Jihadists in America," George Washington University Program on Extremism (November 2016): 11, http:// extremism.gwu.edu/sites/g/files/zaxdzs2191/f/downloads/Female%20Jihadists%20 in%20America.pdf.

12. Katharina Von Knop, "The Female Jihad: Al Qaeda's Women," *Studies in Conflict and Terrorism* 30, no. 5 (2007): 397–414, http://doi.org/10.1080/10576100701258585; V. Arianti and Nur Azlin Yasin, "Women's Proactive Roles in Jihadism in Southeast Asia," *Counter Terrorist Trends and Analyses* 8, no. 5 (May 2016): 9–15, http://jstor.org /stable/26351417; Unaesah Rahmah, "The Role of Women of the Islamic State in the Dynamics of Terrorism in Indonesia," Middle East Institute, May 10, 2016, http:// mei.edu/publications/role-women-islamic-state-dynamics-terrorism-indonesia.

13. Meredith Loken, "Women in War: Militancy, Legitimacy, and Rebel Success" (PhD diss., University of Washington, 2018), http://hdl.handle.net/1773/42520; Alex Braithwaite and Luna B. Ruiz, "Female Combatants, Forced Recruitment, and Civil Conflict Outcomes," *Research and Politics* 5, no. 2 (April–June 2018), http://doi.org /10.1177%2F2053168018770559.

14. Betty A. Dobratz and Stephanie L. Shanks-Meile, "The White Separatist Movement: Worldviews on Gender, Feminism, Nature, and Change," in *Home-Grown Hate: Gender and Organized Racism*, ed. Abby L. Ferber (New York: Routledge, 2004): 123; Blee, "Women and Organized Racial Terrorism," 426.

15. Jessica Trisko Darden, "Female Terrorists: On the Front Lines and Behind the Scenes," *AEIdeas*, February 8, 2019, http://aei.org/publication/female-terrorists-on-the -frontlines-and-behind-the-scenes; Mohammed M. Hafez, "The Ties That Bind: How Terrorists Exploit Family Bonds," *CTC Sentinel* 9, no. 2 (February 2016), https:// ctc.usma.edu/the-ties-that-bind-how-terrorists-exploit-family-bonds.

16. Joana Cook and Gina Vale, "From Daesh to 'Diaspora': Tracing the Women and Minors of Islamic State," International Center for the Study of Radicalisation, King's College London (2018), http://icsr.info/wp-content/uploads/2018/07/ICSR-Report

-From-Daesh-to-%E2%80%98Diaspora%E2%80%99-Tracing-the-Women-and
-Minors-of-Islamic-State.pdf.

17. Kiriloi M. Ingram, "More Than 'Jihadi Brides' and 'Eye Candy': How Dabiq Appeals
to Western Women," International Center for Counter-Terrorism (August 12, 2016),
http://icct.nl/publication/more-than-jihadi-brides-and-eye-candy-how-dabiq-appeals
-to-western-women.

18. Carolyn Hoyle, Alexandra Bradford, and Ross Frenett, "Becoming Mulan?: Female
Western Migrants to ISIS," Institute for Strategic Dialogue (2015): 13, http://
isdglobal.org/wp-content/uploads/2016/02/ISDJ2969_Becoming_Mulan_01.15
_WEB.pdf; Dallin Van Leuven, Dyan Mazurana, and Rachel Gordon, "Analysing
the Recruitment and Use of Foreign Men and Women in ISIL Through a Gender
Perspective," in Foreign Fighters Under International Law and Beyond, ed. Andrea de
Guttry, Francesca Capone, and Christophe Paulussen (The Hague: Asser Press, 2016),
109, http://dx.doi.org/10.1007/978-94-6265-099-2_7.

19. Cook and Vale, "From Daesh to 'Diaspora,'" 14.

20. Pedro Manrique et al., "Women's Connectivity in Extreme Networks," Science Advances
2, no. 6 (June 10, 2016), http://advances.sciencemag.org/content/2/6/e1501742.

21. Milton-Edwards and Attia, "Female Terrorists."

22. Hernandez and Hegarty, "Made-Up to Look Beautiful."

23. Cook and Vale, "From Daesh to 'Diaspora'"; Jayne Huckerby, "When Human
Trafficking and Terrorism Connect: Dangers and Dilemmas," Just Security, February
22, 2019, http://justsecurity.org/62658/human-trafficking-terrorism-connect-dangers
-dilemmas; Helen Stenger and Jacqui True, "Female Foreign Fighters and the Need
for a Gendered Approach to Countering Violent Extremism," Strategist, Australian
Strategic Policy Institute, March 7, 2019, http://aspistrategist.org.au/female-foreign
-fighters-and-the-need-for-a-gendered-approach-to-countering-violent-extremism.

24. Matfess, Women and the War on Boko Haram; Adaobi Tricia Nwaubani, "The Women
Rescued From Boko Haram Who Are Returning to Their Captors," New Yorker,
December 20, 2018, http://newyorker.com/news/dispatch/the-women-rescued-from
-boko-haram-who-are-returning-to-their-captors.

25. Rachel Bryson, "The Complex Challenge of Female ISIS Returnees," Tony Blair
Institute for Global Change, March 7, 2018, http://institute.global/insight/co-existence
/complex-challenge-female-isis-returnees; "Gender Dimensions of the Response to
Returning Foreign Terrorist Fighters: Research Perspectives," UN Security Council
Counter-Terrorism Committee Executive Directorate (February 2019), http://un.org
/sc/ctc/wp-content/uploads/2019/02/Feb_2019_CTED_Trends_Report.pdf; Cook and
Vale, "From Daesh to 'Diaspora'"; Tim Meko, "Now That the Islamic State Has Fallen in
Iraq and Syria, Where Are All Its Fighters Going?," Washington Post, February 22, 2018,
http://washingtonpost.com/graphics/2018/world/isis-returning-fighters.

26. Audrey Alexander and Rebecca Turkington, "Treatment of Terrorists: How Does
Gender Affect Justice?" CTC Sentinel 11, no. 8 (September 2018), https://ctc.usma.edu
/treatment-terrorists-gender-affect-justice; Ester E.J. Strommen, "Jihadi Brides or
Female Foreign Fighters? Women in Da'esh—From Recruitment to Sentencing," GPS
Policy Brief, Peace Research Institute Oslo (2017), http://prio.org/utility/DownloadFile
.ashx?id=1219&type=publicationfile.

27. Leonie Vrugtman, "The Challenge of Female ISIS Returnees in the Balkans," *Global Risk Insights*, July 20, 2018, http://globalriskinsights.com/2018/07/isis-female-returnees-worry-balkans-europe.

28. Alexandra Lily Kather and Anne Schroeter, "Co-opting Universal Jurisdiction? A Gendered Critique of the Prosecutorial Strategy of the German Federal Public Prosecutor in Response to the Return of Female ISIL Members," *OpinoJuris*, March 7, 2019, http://opiniojuris.org/2019/03/07/co-opting-universal-jurisdiction-a-gendered-critique-of-the-prosecutorial-strategy-of-the-german-federal-public-prosecutor-in-response-to-the-return-of-female-isil-members-part-i.

29. "Iraq: Change Approach to Foreign Women, Children in ISIS-Linked Trials," Human Rights Watch, June 21, 2018, http://hrw.org/news/2018/06/21/iraq-change-approach-foreign-women-children-isis-linked-trials.

30. Wenche Iren Hauge, "Disarmament, Demobilization, and Reintegration Processes (DDR): The Gender Asset," GPS Policy Brief, Peace Research Institute Oslo (2015), http://prio.org/utility/DownloadFile.ashx?id=103&type=publicationfile.

31. Kiran Stallone and Julia Zulver, "The Feminists of FARC: 'We Are Not Demobilising, We Are Mobilising Politically,'" *Guardian*, March 27, 2017, http://theguardian.com/lifeandstyle/2017/mar/27/feminists-farc-colombia-female-inequality; Miranda Alison, "Cogs in the Wheel?"

32. Hilary Matfess, "Rescued and Deradicalised Women Are Returning to Boko Haram. Why?," *African Arguments*, November 1, 2017, http://africanarguments.org/2017/11/01/rescued-and-deradicalised-women-are-returning-to-boko-haram-why; Jessica Trisko Darden, Alexis Henshaw, and Ora Szekely, *Insurgent Women: Female Combatants in Civil Wars* (Washington, DC: Georgetown University Press, 2019); "Las Cifras de los 10 Años de Desmovilizaciones," *El Tiempo*, http://eltiempo.com/Multimedia/especiales/desmovilizados/ARCHIVO/ARCHIVO-12224321-0.pdf.

33. Matfess, "Rescued and Deradicalised Women"; Nimmi Gowrinathan, "The Missing Politics of Female Empowerment," *Stanford Social Innovation Review* (Fall 2018), http://ssir.org/articles/entry/the_missing_politics_of_female_empowerment; Kanisha D. Bond et al., "The West Needs to Take the Politics of Women in ISIS Seriously," *Foreign Policy*, March 4, 2019, http://foreignpolicy.com/2019/03/04/the-west-needs-to-take-the-politics-of-women-in-isis-seriously.

34. Stenger and True, "Female Foreign Fighters"; Huckerby, "When Human Trafficking."

35. Rebecca Turkington and Agathe Christien, "Women, Deradicalization, and Rehabilitation: Lessons From an Expert Workshop," Georgetown Institute for Women, Peace and Security (April 2018): 4, http://giwps.georgetown.edu/wp-content/uploads/2018/04/Policy-Brief-Women-Deradicalization-and-Rehabilitation.pdf.

36. Gayle Tzemach Lemmon, "The ISIS Bride Problem: Don't Take It Out on the Children," CNN, April 20, 2018, http://cnn.com/2018/04/20/opinions/isis-bride-children-opinion-lemmon/index.html.

37. Martin Chulov, "Up to 3,000 ISIS Children Living in 'Extremely Dire Conditions,'" *Guardian*, March 13, 2019, http://theguardian.com/world/2019/mar/13/up-to-3000-children-born-to-isis-families-housed-in-dire-conditions.

38. Cook and Vale, "From Daesh to 'Diaspora'"; Meko, "Now That the Islamic State Has Fallen."

39. Karima Bennoune, *Your Fatwa Does Not Apply Here: Untold Stories From the Fight Against Muslim Fundamentalism* (New York: W. W. Norton, 2013); Marie O'Reilly, "Inclusive Security and Peaceful Societies: Exploring the Evidence," *PRISM* 6, no. 1 (2016), http://inclusivesecurity.org/publication/inclusive-security-and-peaceful -societies-exploring-the-evidence; Valerie Hudson et. al, "The Heart of the Matter: The Security of Women and the Security of States," *International Security* 33, No. 3 (2008/2009), http://mitpressjournals.org/doi/pdf/10.1162/isec.2009.33.3.7.

40. Wazhma Frogh, "Imagine If the Minister Had Listened to Us" (speech, Inclusive Security, October 15, 2015), video, 2:28, http://inclusivesecurity.org/2016/04/14 /imagine-minister-listened-us.

41. Swanee Hunt, Esther Ibanga, and Alaa Murabit, "On GPS: Women Waging Peace," interview by Fareed Zakaria, *Fareed Zakaria GPS*, CNN, January 4, 2016, video, 7:50, http://cnn.com/videos/tv/2016/01/04/exp-gps-0103-hunt-ibanga-murabit.cnn; Anne-Marie Slaughter and Elizabeth Weingarten, "A National Security Blind Spot," *Straits Times*, October 28, 2016, http://straitstimes.com/opinion/a-national-security-blind -spot.

42. Louise Olsson and Johan Tejpar, eds., *Operational Effectiveness and UN Resolution 1325—Practices and Lessons From Afghanistan* (Stockholm: FOI, 2009), 117, 126–127; Tobie Whitman and Jacqueline O'Neill, "Attention to Gender Increases Security in Operations: Examples From the North Atlantic Treaty Organization (NATO)," The Institute for Inclusive Security (April 2012): 7–13, http://inclusivesecurity.org/wp -content/uploads/2013/05/NATO-Report_8.pdf.

43. Kim Lonsway et al., "Policy Briefing Paper: Gender Sensitive Police Reform in Post Conflict Societies," UN Development Fund for Women and UN Development Program (October 2007), http://unwomen.org/~/media/Headquarters/Media/Publications /UNIFEM/GenderSensitivePoliceReformPolicyBrief2007eng.pdf; Tara Denham, "Police Reform and Gender," Geneva Center for the Democratic Control of Armed Forces (DCAF) (2008): 5, http://dcaf.ch/police-reform-and-gender-tool-2.

44. Maja Daruwala and Devika Prasad, eds., *Rough Roads to Equality: Women Policy in South Asia* (New Delhi: Commonwealth Human Rights Initiative, 2015), http:// humanrightsinitiative.org/download/1449728344rough-roads-to-equalitywomen -police-in-south-asia-august-2015.pdf; *The World's Women 2015: Trends and Statistics* (New York: United Nations, 2015), http://unstats.un.org/unsd/gender/downloads /worldswomen2015_report.pdf.

45. "Preventing Extremism in Fragile States: A New Approach," Task Force on Extremism in Fragile States, U.S. Institute of Peace (February 2019), http://usip.org/publications /2019/02/preventing-extremism-fragile-states-new-approach.

46. *The Role of Civil Society in Preventing and Countering Violent Extremism and Radicalization That Lead to Terrorism: A Focus on South-Eastern Europe* (Vienna: Organization for Security and Cooperation in Europe, 2018), http://osce.org /secretariat/400241.

47. Dina Temple-Raston, "The Female Quran Experts Fighting Radical Islam in

Morocco," *Atlantic*, February 12, 2018, http://theatlantic.com/international/archive/2018/02/the-female-quran-experts-fighting-radical-islam-in-morocco/551996.

48. Joyce Hackel, "'It's Not About You Being a Muslim and Me Being a Christian,' Says One Nigerian Activist," PRI, January 14, 2015, http://pri.org/stories/2015-01-14/its-not-about-you-being-muslim-and-me-being-christian-says-one-nigerian-activist.

49. Krithika Varagur, "Empowering Women to Break the Jihadi Cycle," *New York Times*, June 20, 2017, http://nytimes.com/2017/06/20/opinion/empowering-women-to-break-the-jihadi-cycle.html.

50. Fionnuala Ni Aolain and Jayne Huckerby, "Gendering Counterterrorism: How To, and How Not To," *Just Security*, May 1, 2018, http://justsecurity.org/55522/gendering-counterterrorism-to.

51. "Tightening the Purse Strings: What Countering Terrorism Financing Costs Gender Equality and Security," Duke Law International Human Rights Clinic and Women Peacemakers Program (March 2017), http://law.duke.edu/sites/default/files/humanrights/tighteningpursestrings.pdf.

52. "Tightening the Purse Strings," Duke Law International Human Rights Clinic and Women Peacemakers Program.

53. "Trafficking in Persons Report," U.S. Department of State (June 2018), http://state.gov/documents/organization/282798.pdf.

54. "Trafficking in Persons Report," U.S. Department of State (June 2017), http://state.gov/documents/organization/271339.pdf.

55. Erin Marie Saltman and Melanie Smith, "'Till Martyrdom Do Us Part': Gender and the ISIS Phenomenon," Institute for Strategic Dialogue (2015), http://isdglobal.org/wp-content/uploads/2016/02/Till_Martyrdom_Do_Us_Part_Gender_and_the_ISIS_Phenomenon.pdf.

56. "Letter Dated 27 October 2014 From the Chair of the Security Council Committee Pursuant to Resolutions 1267 (1999) and 1989 (2011) Concerning Al-Qaida and Associated Individuals and Entities Addressed to the President of the Security Council," UN Security Council, S/2-14/770, http://un.org/ga/search/view_doc.asp?symbol=S/2014/770.

57. "'Those Terrible Weeks in Their Camp,'" Human Rights Watch, October 27, 2014, http://hrw.org/report/2014/10/27/those-terrible-weeks-their-camp/boko-haram-violence-against-women-and-girls.

58. Gaffey, "ISIS Just Started Using Female Suicide Bombers."

59. "UN: Sexual Violence Increasingly Used as 'Terrorism' Tactic," Associated Press, May 16, 2017, http://news24.com/World/News/un-sexual-violence-increasingly-used-as-terrorism-tactic-20170516; Dara Kay Cohen, "Explaining Rape During Civil War: Cross-National Evidence (1980–2009)," *American Political Science Review* 107, no. 3 (August 2013): 461–477.

60. Heather Hurlburt and Jacqueline O'Neill, "We Need to Think Harder About Terrorism and Gender. ISIS Already Is," *Vox*, June 21, 2017, http://vox.com/the-big-idea/2017/6/1/15722746/terrorism-gender-women-manchester-isis-counterterrorism.

61. Amanda Taub, "Control and Fear: What Mass Killings and Domestic Violence Have in Common," *New York Times*, June 15, 2016, http://nytimes.com/2016/06/16/world /americas/control-and-fear-what-mass-killings-and-domestic-violence-have-in-common .html; "Guns and Domestic Violence," Everytown for Gun Safety Support Fund, http:// everytownresearch.org/guns-domestic-violence.

62. "Addressing the Needs of Women Affected by Armed Conflict: An ICRC Guidance Document," International Committee of the Red Cross (2004), http://icrc.org/eng /assets/files/other/icrc_002_0840_women_guidance.pdf; Elisabeth Jean Wood, "Conflict-Related Sexual Violence and the Policy Implications of Recent Research," *International Review of the Red Cross*, 2015, http://icrc.org/en/international-review /article/conflict-related-sexual-violence-and-policy-implications-recent.

63. Stephanie Sinclair, "Child, Bride, Mother: Nigeria," *New York Times*, January 27, 2017, http://nytimes.com/interactive/2017/01/27/sunday-review/29Exposures-child-bride -interactive.html; Kimberly Theidon, "Hidden in Plain Sight: Children Born of Wartime Sexual Violence," Open Democracy, September 30, 2015, http://opendemocracy.net /opensecurity/kimberly-theidon/hidden-in-plain-sight-children-born-of-wartime -sexual-violence.

64. Anke Hoeffler and James Fearon, "Post-2015 Consensus: Conflict and Violence Assessment," Copenhagen Consensus Center (2015), http://copenhagenconsensus .com/publication/post-2015-consensus-conflict-and-violence-assessment-hoeffler -fearon.

65. Rukmini Callimachi, "ISIS Enshrines a Theology of Rape," *New York Times*, August 13, 2015, http://nytimes.com/2015/08/14/world/middleeast/isis-enshrines-a-theology -of-rape.html.

66. Michael Kimmel, "Almost All Violent Extremists Share One Thing: Their Gender," *Guardian*, April 8, 2018, http://theguardian.com/world/2018/apr/08/violent-extremists -share-one-thing-gender-michael-kimmel.

67. Valerie M. Hudson and Hilary Matfess, "In Plain Sight: The Neglected Linkage Between Brideprice and Violent Conflict," *International Security* 42, no. 1 (Summer 2017): 7–40, http://www.armyupress.army.mil/Portals/7/Hot%20Spots/Documents /Gender/Hudson%201.pdf.

68. "Women's Perceptions of the Afghan National Police," Samuel Hall Consulting (2011): 19, http://samuelhall.org/wp-content/uploads/2011/12/Gender-Dynamics-of-Kabul -Women-and-Police.pdf.

69. Cornelius Friesendorf, "Paramilitarization and Security Sector Reform: The Afghan National Police," *International Peacekeeping* 18, no. 1 (January 26, 2011): 79–95, http://doi.org/10.1080/13533312.2011.527517.

70. John S. McCain National Defense Authorization Act for Fiscal Year 2019, Pub. L. No. 1, 2018.

71. Sophia Jones, "The Many Dangers of Being an Afghan Woman in Uniform," *New York Times* magazine, October 5, 2018, http://nytimes.com/2018/10/05/magazine /afghanistan-women-security-forces.html.

72. "Strengthening the Afghan National Police: Recruitment and Retention of Women Officers," Japan International Cooperation Agency and Georgetown Institute for

Women, Peace, and Security (2016), http://giwps.georgetown.edu/wp-content/uploads/2017/08/Strengthening-the-Afghan-National-Police-Recruitment-and-Retention-of-Women-Officers.pdf.

73. Jones, "The Many Dangers."

74. Hernandez and Hegarty, "Made-Up to Look Beautiful."

75. Gaffey, "ISIS Just Started Using Female Suicide Bombers"; Hernandez and Hegarty, "Made-Up to Look Beautiful"; Warner and Matfess, "Exploding Stereotypes."

76. Nwaubani, "The Women Rescued From Boko Haram"; Azadeh Moaveni, "What Would Make a Woman Go Back to Boko Haram? Despair," *Guardian*, January 14, 2019, http://theguardian.com/commentisfree/2019/jan/14/woman-boko-haram-nigeria-militant-group.

77. "Invisible Women: Gendered Dimensions of Return, Rehabilitation and Reintegration From Violent Extremism," International Civil Society Action Network and UN Development Program (2019): 94, http://icanpeacework.org/wp-content/uploads/2019/02/ICAN-UNDP-Rehabilitation-Reintegration-Invisible-Women-Report-2019.pdf.

78. Theidon, "Hidden in Plain Sight."

79. "Invisible Women," 75; "How Hamsatu Allamin Changed Boko Haram to Boko Halal in Nigeria," International Civil Society Action Network, January 8, 2018, http://icanpeacework.org/2018/01/08/hamsatu-allamin-nigeria.

80. "Invisible Women," 96.

81. Malcolm Sutton, *Bear in Mind These Dead: An Index of Deaths From the Conflict in Ireland 1969–1993* (Belfast: Beyond the Pale Publications, 1994).

82. Margaret Ward, *Unmanageable Revolutionaries: Women and Irish Nationalism* (London: Pluto Press, 1989).

83. Mia Bloom, *Bombshell: Women and Terrorism* (Philadelphia: University of Pennsylvania Press, 2011), 70.

84. Helen Harris, "Everyday Resistance," in *Strong About It All: Rural and Urban Women's Experiences of the Security Forces in Northern Ireland*, ed. Helen Harris and Eileen Healy (Belfast: North West Women's/Human Rights Project, 2001), 66.

85. Sandra McEvoy, "Loyalist Women Paramilitaries in Northern Ireland: Beginning a Feminist Conversation About Conflict Resolution," *Security Studies* 18, no. 2 (May 2009): 269, http://doi.org/10.1080/09636410902900095.

86. Marie Hammond-Callaghan, "'Peace Women,' Gender and Peacebuilding in Northern Ireland: From Reconciliation and Political Inclusion to Human Rights and Human Security," in *Building Peace in Northern Ireland*, ed. Maria Power (Liverpool: Liverpool University Press, 2011), 93–111, http://doi.org/10.5949/UPO9781846316739.006.

87. Patty Chang et al., "Women Leading Peace: A Close Examination of Women's Political Participation in Peace Processes in Northern Ireland, Guatemala, Kenya, and the Philippines," Georgetown Institute for Women, Peace, and Security (2015), http://giwps.georgetown.edu/wp-content/uploads/2017/08/Women-Leading-Peace.pdf.

88. Seyward Darby, "The Rise of the Valkyries," *Harper's* (September 2017), http:// harpers.org/archive/2017/09/the-rise-of-the-valkyries; Kanisha D. Bond, "Women's Participation and the Institutional Design of Violent Political Organizations" (working paper, 2015).

89. Pat St. Claire, Greg Botelho, and Ralph Ellis, "San Bernardino Shooter Tashfeen Malik: Who Was She?" CNN, December 8, 2018, http://cnn.com/2015/12/06/us /san-bernardino-shooter-tashfeen-malik/index.html.

90. Audrey Alexander, ed., "Perspectives on the Future of Women, Gender, and Violent Extremism," Program on Extremism, George Washington University (February 2019): 37, http://extremism.gwu.edu/sites/g/files/zaxdzs2191/f/Perspectives%20 on%20the%20Future%20of%20Women%2C%20Gender%20and%20Violent%20 Extremism.pdf.

91. Alexander Meleagrou-Hitchens, Seamus Hughes, and Bennett Clifford, "The Travelers: American Jihadists in Syria and Iraq," Program on Extremism, George Washington University (February 2018): 86, http://extremism.gwu.edu/sites/g/files /zaxdzs2191/f/TravelersAmericanJihadistsinSyriaandIraq.pdf.

92. Meleagrou-Hitchens, "The Travelers."

93. Alexander and Turkington, "Treatment of Terrorists"; "Profiles of Individual Radicalization in the United States (PIRUS)," START: National Consortium for the Study of Terrorism and Responses to Terrorism, University of Maryland, http:// start.umd.edu/data-tools/profiles-individual-radicalization-united-states-pirus.

94. Alexander and Turkington, "Treatment of Terrorists."

95. Robert Windrem, "Sisterhood of Spies: Women Now Hold the Top Positions at the CIA," NBC News, January 5, 2019, http://nbcnews.com/news/us-news/all-three-cia -directorates-will-now-be-headed-women-n954956; Robert Windrem, "Sisterhood of Spies: Women Crack the Code at the CIA," NBC News, November 14, 2013, http:// nbcnews.com/news/world/sisterhood-spies-women-crack-code-cia-flna2D11594601.

96. Robert Windrem, "Hunting Osama bin Laden Was Women's Work," NBC News, November 14, 2013, http://nbcnews.com/news/world/hunting-osama-bin-laden-was -womens-work-flna2D11594091.

97. Ian Shapira, "For CIA Family, a Deadly Suicide Bombing Leads to Painful Divisions," *Washington Post*, January 28, 2012, http://washingtonpost.com/local/for-cia-family -a-deadly-suicide-bombing-leads-to-painful-divisions/2012/01/20/gIQAyJGVYQ _story.html; Richard A. Oppel Jr., "Her Title: Cryptologic Technician. Her Occupation: Warrior," *New York Times*, February 8, 2019, http://nytimes.com/2019/02/08/us /shannon-kent-military-spy.html.

98. "Our Programs," Life After Hate, http://lifeafterhate.org/programs.

99. "Department of State and USAID Joint Strategy on Countering Violent Extremism," U.S. Department of State and USAID (May 2016), https://pdf.usaid.gov/pdf_docs /PBAAE503.pdf.

100. Kristy N. Kamarck, "Diversity, Inclusion, and Equal Opportunity in the Armed Services: Background and Issues for Congress," Congressional Research Service (December 23, 2016), http://fas.org/sgp/crs/natsec/R44321.pdf.

101. "The Role of Families in Preventing and Countering Violent Extremism: Strategic Recommendations and Programming Options," Global Counterterrorism Forum Countering Violent Extremism (CVE) Working Group (September 2015), http://thegctf.org/Portals/1/Documents/Toolkit-documents/English-The-Role-of-Familes-in-PCVE.pdf; "Good Practices on Women and Countering Violent Extremism," Global Counterterrorism Forum (2014), https://thegctf.org/Portals/1/Documents/Framework%20Documents/A/GCTF-Good-Practices-on-Women-and-CVE.pdf.

102. "Arab League Presents Regional Action Plan for Women, Peace and Security," UN Women, October 13, 2015, http://arabstates.unwomen.org/en/news/stories/2015/10/arab-league-presents-regional-action-plan.

103. Rosalie Fransen et al., "National Action Plans on Preventing Violent Extremism: A Gendered Content Analysis," International Civil Society Action Network (Fall 2017), http://icanpeacework.org/wp-content/uploads/2017/09/GSX-2017-PVE-NAPs-Analysis-1.pdf.

104. Fransen et al., "National Action Plans."

105. Jane Arraf, "Freed From ISIS, Few Yazidis Return to Suffering Families, Many Remain Missing," NPR, March 14, 2019, http://npr.org/2019/03/14/702650912/freed-from-isis-few-yazidis-return-to-suffering-families-many-remain-missing.

106. Lindsay Geller, "How Comedic YouTube Videos Are Being Used to Counter Violent Extremism," *A Plus*, July 2, 2018, http://aplus.com/a/priyank-mathur-mythos-labs-youtube-terrorism.

107. Jennifer Philippa Eggert, "The Roles of Women in Counter-Radicalisation and Disengagement (CRaD) Processes: Best Practices and Lessons Learned From Europe and the Arab World," Berghof Foundation (2018), http://berghof-foundation.org/fileadmin/redaktion/Publications/Other_Resources/Berghof_Input_Paper_Women_Counterradicalisation.pdf.

108. Rosabeth Moss Kanter, *Men and Women of the Corporation* (New York: Basic Books, 1997), 381–395.

109. Amy E. Cunningham and Khalid Koser, "Why Preventing Violent Extremism is the Private Sector's Business," in *Global Terrorism Index*, Institute for Economics and Peace (2016): 79–81, http://economicsandpeace.org/wp-content/uploads/2016/11/Global-Terrorism-Index-2016.2.pdf.

110. Bond, "Women's Participation."

ACKNOWLEDGMENTS

This report was produced under the guidance of CFR's Advisory Committee on Women and Preventing Terrorism, a distinguished group of experts from the government, multilateral organizations, academia, and the private and public sectors. Over the past several months, members of this advisory committee have participated in meetings, reviewed drafts, and shared research and insights from their work. The report has been enhanced considerably by the expertise of this advisory group, and we are thankful for members' participation. The views expressed here and any errors are our own.

A special acknowledgment is extended to James M. Lindsay, CFR's director of studies, for his support for this project, and Bruce Hoffman and Farah Pandith, CFR senior fellows, for their partnership in this effort. We are grateful to Patricia Dorff, Julie Hersh, and Chloe Moffett for their review of previous drafts, and to Rebecca Turkington for her expert insight and Alexandra Bro for her excellent assistance in the production of this paper. U.S. officials also provided feedback that significantly contributed to the report.

This report was written under the auspices of the Women and Foreign Policy program, and was made possible by the generous support of the Compton Foundation.

Jamille Bigio
Rachel Vogelstein

ABOUT THE AUTHORS

Jamille Bigio is a senior fellow in the Women and Foreign Policy program at the Council on Foreign Relations. Previously, she was director for human rights and gender on the White House National Security Council staff and advised First Lady Michelle Obama on adolescent girls' education. From 2009 to 2013, Bigio was senior advisor to the U.S. Ambassador-at-Large for Global Women's Issues at the Department of State, and was detailed to the office of the undersecretary of defense for policy and to the U.S. Mission to the African Union. Bigio led the interagency launch of the U.S. National Action Plan on Women, Peace, and Security, an effort for which she was recognized with the U.S. Department of State Superior Honor Award and the U.S. Department of Defense Secretary of Defense Honor Award. Bigio graduated from the University of Maryland and received her master's degree from the Harvard Kennedy School.

Rachel Vogelstein is the Douglas Dillon senior fellow and director of the Women and Foreign Policy program at the Council on Foreign Relations. From 2009 to 2012, Vogelstein was director of policy and senior advisor within the office of U.S. Secretary of State Hillary Rodham Clinton, and represented the U.S. Department of State as a member of the White House Council on Women and Girls. Previously, Vogelstein was the director of the women and girls programs in the office of Hillary Clinton at the Clinton Foundation, where she oversaw the development of the No Ceilings initiative and provided guidance on domestic and global women's issues. Prior to joining the State Department, Vogelstein was senior counsel at the National Women's Law Center in Washington, DC, where she specialized in women's health and reproductive rights. Vogelstein is a recipient of the U.S.

Department of State Superior Honor Award and the National Women Lawyer's Award. She graduated from Columbia University's Barnard College and received a law degree from Georgetown Law School.

ADVISORY COMMITTEE
Women and Terrorism

Fatima Akilu
Neem Foundation

Bruce Hoffman, *ex officio*
Council on Foreign Relations

Jayne Huckerby
Duke University School of Law

Adnan Kifayat
Gen Next Foundation

Nancy Lindborg
U.S. Institute of Peace

Lisa Monaco
New York University School of Law

Rasa Ostrauskaite
*Organization for Security and
Cooperation in Europe*

Farah Pandith, *ex officio*
Council on Foreign Relations

Leon Panetta
*The Panetta Institute for
Public Policy; Former Secretary
of Defense*

Mossarat Qadeem
PAIMAN Alumni Trust

Frances Townsend
MacAndrews & Forbes, Inc.

Jacqui True
Monash University

Lorenzo Vidino
George Washington University

Juan Zarate
*Center for Strategic and
International Studies*

This report reflects the judgments and recommendations of the authors. It does not necessarily represent the views of members of the advisory committee, whose involvement should in no way be interpreted as an endorsement of the report by either themselves or the organizations with which they are affiliated.